FAST FOOD

DAVID

**BIBLE CHARACTER STUDIES
FOR PRE-TEENS**

BY DARREN

First published in 1998 by
KEVIN MAYHEW LTD
Rattlesden
Bury St Edmunds
Suffolk IP30 0SZ

© 1998 Darren

The right of Darren to be identified as the author
of this work has been asserted by him in accordance
with the Copyright, Designs and Patents Act 1988.

All rights reserved. No part of this publication may be reproduced,
stored in a retrieval system, or transmitted, in any form or by any means,
electronic, mechanical, photocopying, recording or otherwise,
without the prior written permission of the publisher.

All artwork in this book may be photocopied without copyright infringement,
provided it is used for the purpose for which the book is intended.
Reproduction of any of the contents of this book for commercial purposes
is subject to the usual copyright restrictions.

Scripture quotations taken from the Holy Bible, New International Version.
Copyright © 1973, 1978, 1984 by International Bible Society.
Used by permission of Hodder & Stoughton Limited.
All rights reserved.

0 1 2 3 4 5 6 7 8 9

ISBN 1 84003 142 5
Catalogue No 1500163

Cover by Darren
Edited by David Gatward
Typesetting by Louise Hill
Printed in Great Britain

Contents

	Introduction	5
Episode 1	Samuel Anoints David	7
Episode 2	David Defeats Goliath	15
Episode 3	David, Jonathan and Saul	23
Episode 4	David Spares Saul's Life	31
Episode 5	David and the Death of Saul	39
Episode 6	David Praises the Lord	47
Episode 7	God's Amazing Promise	55
Episode 8	David's Dreadful Sins	63
Episode 9	David and Absalom	71
Episode 10	David and the Temple	79
Episode 11	What We Have Learned from David	87

FAST FOOD SERIES

JOSEPH
DAVID

Look out for further titles

Introduction

Everybody knows the story of David and Goliath, but how many people (particularly children) know much about the rebellion of his son Absalom? Both are major events in the story of David containing lessons and examples as relevant to us today as any other Bible story – the only difference is that one is a well-known and immediately accessible section in the story of David's life, whilst the other is rarely looked at. Such is the case with so many well-known Bible characters – large sections of their life's story are familiar to us yet little or nothing is often known of the times before, after or in between!

The aim of these books is to try and provide as full and complete a study as possible on specific characters, looking at their life in sequence from beginning to end, drawing attention to the events that shaped them, the development of their relationship with, and understanding of, God, and the unfolding of God's will and promises in their lives.

Obviously, with some stories spanning many books of the Bible, not every detail can be included but I hope that I have been as thorough as is practical! I believe these studies will enable children to appreciate and relate to the characters on a deeper level with an awareness of the bigger picture – an understanding of their life and attitudes as a whole, not just as isolated segments.

How to use these books

Each book is divided into eleven sections – ten character studies, with a review in the eleventh. Each section contains one lesson plan, three overhead sheets, one in-class worksheet and one take-home sheet. (I hope that there will be more than enough material for each session – far better to have to leave some out than be left short and have to make some up!)

Lesson plan

Before arriving at the lesson, make sure you've read the complete lesson plan! It may seem obvious but making sure you understand and agree with the contents will help you as you lead the meeting.

Each lesson plan begins with a Bible reading (or a Background Information section where necessary, to be read out first). All readings and verses throughout these books are taken from the NIV Bible, unless otherwise stated. The verses that correspond to the overhead pictures are listed in order so that the picture can be placed up when the verse is reached.

The main teaching on the reading is in the form of questions to be read out to the children and 'desired answers'. Make sure you have read the desired answers and lesson summaries and then, bearing those answers in mind, gently lead the discussion and the children's responses introducing the given answers along the way. (The answers are written in such a way that they can be read out if discussion proves difficult at times.)

Helpful points

- It is most important to encourage the children to think about and understand the story and the questions themselves. Do not step in with the 'answers' too quickly!

- Make sure that the children address each section before moving on – further explanation or re-reading may be necessary.

- Try and involve *all* the children. This may mean addressing the questions to specific individuals, or asking the children if they agree with any opinions offered, etc.

- Above all be encouraging! Make sure they know when they're right but don't feel silly if they're wrong.

- The additional material is there to be used where appropriate or practical. Worksheets are explained where necessary and puzzles that require answers in the take-home sheet are given.

- Each session ends with a prayer that can either be prayed by you or by one of the children.

Overheads There are three overhead illustrations for each section. (If appropriate these can also be photocopied onto plain paper and used as colouring sheets.)

Worksheets These are intended to be completed in lesson time, but most will work equally well as take-home sheets if necessary.

Take-home sheets When answers are needed they are given in the lesson plan. Since the take-home sheets often contain questions relevant to the reading, I suggest that the sheets are brought back completed the following week and the answers given in class. This should encourage the children to complete the readings and questions as well as the puzzles.

I hope that these books prove helpful to you – please write to Kevin Mayhew Publishers with comments, ideas or suggestions that might be included in further work.

EPISODE 1

Samuel Anoints David

EPISODE 1 — Samuel Anoints David

Reading

1 Samuel 16:1-13. Samuel anoints David to be king after Saul.

Overheads

1 (v 6) Samuel considers Eliab.
2 (v 11) David looking after the sheep.
3 (v 13) The anointing.

What this episode tells us

What we can learn from David
Consistent godly living, especially in the ordinary unseen times.

What we can learn about God
God sees our hearts, not just our deeds.

Discussion questions and desired answers

If it was your job to appoint a new prime minister, what kind of things would you look for?
Focus on achievements, leadership qualities, qualifications, etc.

Had David done anything important or noticeable like these?
No.

What did David do?
David simply tended his father's sheep in the fields.

How then do you think God had noticed him?
God had noticed how David was as he went about his everyday duties – his heart, attitudes and motives.

Read 1 Samuel 13:14. What does God call David?
A man after his own heart.

David had been doing nothing special or important in the eyes of man – yet God says this to him! How do you think this is relevant to your life?
Sometimes it may feel like you are not doing anything special or important and so can't be pleasing God, yet God looks at how you do those ordinary and normal things – he sees the heart and the motives.

Can you think of some examples?
The Bible tells us to obey our parents – if you do what they ask willingly, not complaining in your heart, even if it's just washing up or dusting, etc., that is an obedient heart in God's sight.

Can you think of examples that whilst they may appear good, may offend God?

You could give food to a homeless person, not because you cared about them, but because it made you look good in front of your friends.

What do you think is important to remember from today's lesson?

God can always see that one place no one else can – our hearts. No matter what you do, it is how you do it inside that is what God looks for.

Additional material

Further reading

Mark 12:41-44. The rich put large amounts of money in the offering but the poor widow put in only a penny. The appearance was that she gave little, but Jesus saw her heart and knew she was giving everything.

Fun

'Where's That Sheep?' Game. Nominate one person as David, the shepherd. This person stands in the centre of a room with everyone else (the sheep!) all around them. They must then shut their eyes whilst one 'sheep' is nominated and either leaves the room or hides. 'David' must then open his eyes whilst the sheep all move around the room baaing (if desired!). The object of the game is to find which 'sheep' is missing. Take turns at being 'David' and have the guessing timed. The winner being the person who found the missing sheep in the quickest time. This game works better the more people there are to take part; and the more the sheep move around and 'baa', the harder it will be for 'David' to find the missing one!

Worksheet

Self-explanatory (but you will need scissors for the children). If possible, enlarge the jigsaw to A3. It will make the cutting out easier. It may also be helpful to stick the pieces down.

Take-home sheet

The two missing sheep from the first picture are the one half behind the tree on the far left at the back, and the one in the middle foreground, eating grass.

Box: grain. Chest: empty. Pot: gold. Bag: bread. Sack: cloth.

Closing prayer

Father God, thank you that you are interested in me – not for what I do but for who I am inside. You know me completely. I pray, Lord, that when my motives and attitudes are not what they should be, you will help me to see and to change them because I want all of my life – inside and outside – to be pleasing to you. Amen.

Can you cut out the shapes above and fit them over the picture of David? (Take care! Not all the words will be the correct way around on the finished jigsaw!) These are the 'fruits of the Spirit' (as mentioned by Paul in Galatians 5:22-23). This is the sort of thing God would have seen when he looked at David – what was on the inside, not what was on the outside.

'A MAN AFTER GOD'S OWN HEART...'

David has moved the sheep from one field to another but now it seems some have gone missing! Circle the sheep in the first picture that are now missing.

ON THE INSIDE....

On the left are five containers – four of them carry either nothing or fairly ordinary things – but one of them is full of gold! Which one would you expect to find gold in? Using the following clues can you work out what is in each container?

BOX CHEST POT BAG SACK

- the bag holds something edible
- the grain and the bread are not in containers next to each other
- the cloth is in a material container
- the container next to the one carrying gold is empty
- the cloth and the bread are in containers next to each other
- the box is not empty

Read 1 Samuel 16 vs 14-23....
How does King Saul's servant describe David?
_____
_____
_____

What does David do that causes Saul's evil spirit to leave him? _____
_____

Where did you expect the gold to be? Where you thought you may find it depended on which container you thought *looked* best suited to carrying gold. Just like the containers we are all different on the outside, in how we look, how we act, what we do, etc. But God looks at our suitability *inside* – that's what matters.

EPISODE 2

David Defeats Goliath

EPISODE 2

David Defeats Goliath

Reading

1 Samuel 17:32-50.

Background information

The Philistine army is preparing to attack King Saul and the army of Israel. In their army they have a champion – a giant called Goliath who challenges any one of Saul's men to beat him. David was taking food to his brothers in Saul's army when he heard Goliath's challenge.

Overheads

1 (Background) Goliath's challenge.
2 (v 40) David approaches Goliath.
3 (v 49) David's stone strikes Goliath.

What this episode tells us

What we can learn from David
Recognition of what is offensive to God – knowing God's standards.

What we can learn about God
Responds to a stand made in his name.

Discussion questions and desired answers

What does David say when he hears Goliath's defiant challenge to the army of Israel – God's chosen nation?
Have someone read out 1 Samuel 17, verse 26 and verse 45.

What is David feeling?
David is offended by Goliath's open blasphemy.

Why would this offend David?
David knows God – he knows the reverence and respect due to God and the giant's choice to deny this is offensive to him.

David chooses to make a stand against Goliath in defence of God's name. How does God respond to that?
God gives David victory against all the odds! An armed giant against a boy with only a sling!

It is important for us to recognise those things which may be offensive to God because we should want nothing to do with them. Can you think of some examples you could quite easily face?

Encourage relevant and likely examples, e.g. offensive films or music; bullying; deliberate disobedience to parents, teachers, etc.; shoplifting with friends, etc.)

What could you do when you're faced with this sort of situation?

You can choose either to be a part of it or not. David made an open stand against Goliath – sometimes to confront people or to speak out against a situation is the best thing to do – other times it may be better to keep quiet, to walk away, have nothing to do with it, etc.

How do you think you would know how to respond?

Pray to God straight away – ask him to show you how best to act then do what you believe is right – it may not always be easy and sometimes you could even offend your friends, but remember who you could be offending otherwise! Also, God does not overlook a stand made in his name – he didn't let David be harmed and would be there for you in the same way.

Additional material

Further reading

Luke 23:39-43. Of the two thieves crucified with Jesus, one begins to swear at him whilst the other recognises the blasphemy and condemns it. Jesus promises this man a place that day in paradise.

Worksheet

Self-explanatory.

Take-home sheet

Goliath: 'Am I a dog that you come at me with sticks?'

David: 'You come at me with a sword and a spear but I come in the name of the Lord of Israel who you have offended.

Sword, swore, store, stone.

Closing prayer

Dear Lord Jesus, I never want to do anything, or be a part of anything that is offensive to you. Please guide the choices I make and give me the strength I need to follow your ways instead of the world's ways. Thank you that whatever I face, you are there with me.
Amen.

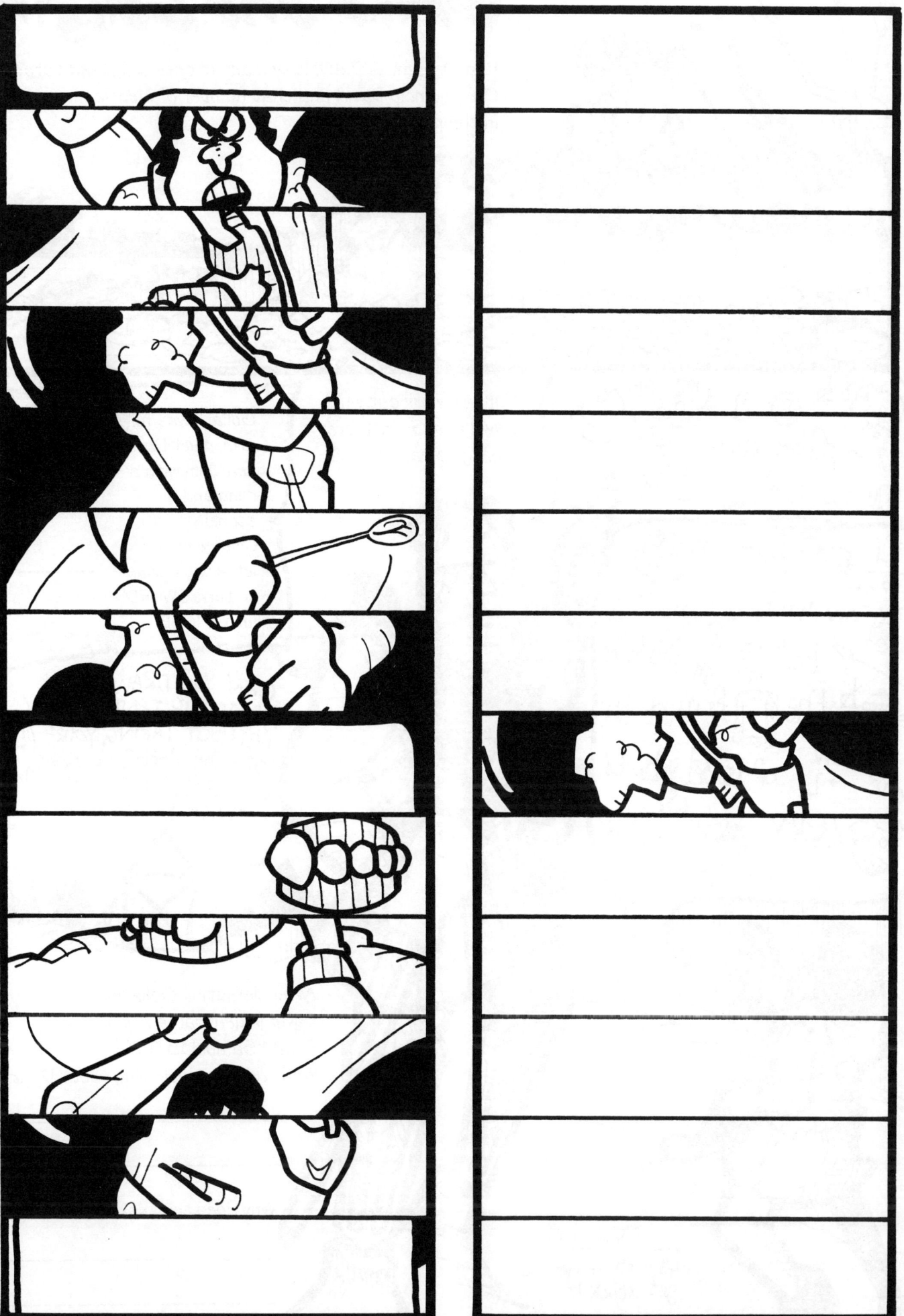

Cut out the pictures on the left and stick them in the correct places on the right to complete the picture of David. Alternatively, they could be copied in the correct spaces instead.

EPISODE 3

David, Jonathan and Saul

EPISODE 3 — David, Jonathan and Saul

Reading

1 Samuel 19:1-12.

Background information

In Saul's household, David finds deep friendship with Jonathan, Saul's eldest son and officially next in line to the throne. Jonathan loved David and recognised God's anointing on him to one day be king – something that only made their relationship stronger. David fought many battles in Saul's army and always had great success because God was with him. The more battles he fought, the more popular he became, and the more Saul grew jealous of him.

Overheads

1. (Background) David and Jonathan – successful in friendship and battle.
2. (v 4) Jonathan speaks with Saul.
3. (v 10) Saul throws his spear at David.

What this episode tells us

What we can learn from David
Honesty with God.

What we can learn about God
He desires to bear our burdens, and is always there for us and to hear us.

Discussion questions and desired answers

David is growing more popular and successful, yet the king is trying to kill him! How do you think David must have felt?

Encourage children to imagine that David knows God has anointed him to one day be king, yet the current anointed one of God – Saul – is trying to kill him when he has done nothing wrong! David must have been confused, fearful, vulnerable, etc.

How do you think David coped?
He turned to God – he prayed and wrote him psalms (songs).

Read Psalm 59:1-4. David wrote this psalm after he had escaped Saul's men through the window of his own house. How does David talk to God here?

Honestly. Throughout the psalms we see David being completely honest with God – he doesn't try to hide his anger, his fear, his happiness, etc. He tells God exactly how he feels.

How is this relevant to our prayers?

In our prayers we can talk to God. If we are worried about something, it's OK to tell him. If we're happy, angry, sad, etc., it is OK to tell God why. He can never be shocked or surprised by our honesty! He already knows our hearts better than we do!

What does David call God in Psalm 59:16?

His fortress.

What does a fortress do?

It protects.

What is David saying?

That at any time in any situation he can turn to God – a safe place where he can be comforted, be honest, be himself and know that God cares.

Additional material

Lesson aid – practical

Encourage children to write, in complete honesty, their hopes, fears, desires, etc., to God. Make sure they know no one else will read it, then ask them to seal it in an envelope with their name. In a year's time, or six months' time, etc., hand them back to the children so that they are able to see how they felt back then, and recognise how God has helped them through whatever worried them, etc. These can be written ideally in lesson time to ensure the teacher is able to collect everything in, but the children's writing could alternatively be completed at home.

Further reading

*Can We Talk, Lord?** – a teenager's honest and real prayers to God – modern psalms of the heart!

Worksheet

Praise be to the Lord, who daily bears our burdens.

Take-home sheet

1 The private room
2 5
3 The guard kitchen
4 8
5 1 – the guard kitchen

Closing prayer

Dear God, thank you so much that there is never a time when I cannot turn to you and there is nothing that I can't share with you. I want my life to be an open book for you to read – please be near to me this week. Amen.

Can We Talk, Lord by David Gatward (1992). Published by Kevin Mayhew Limited.

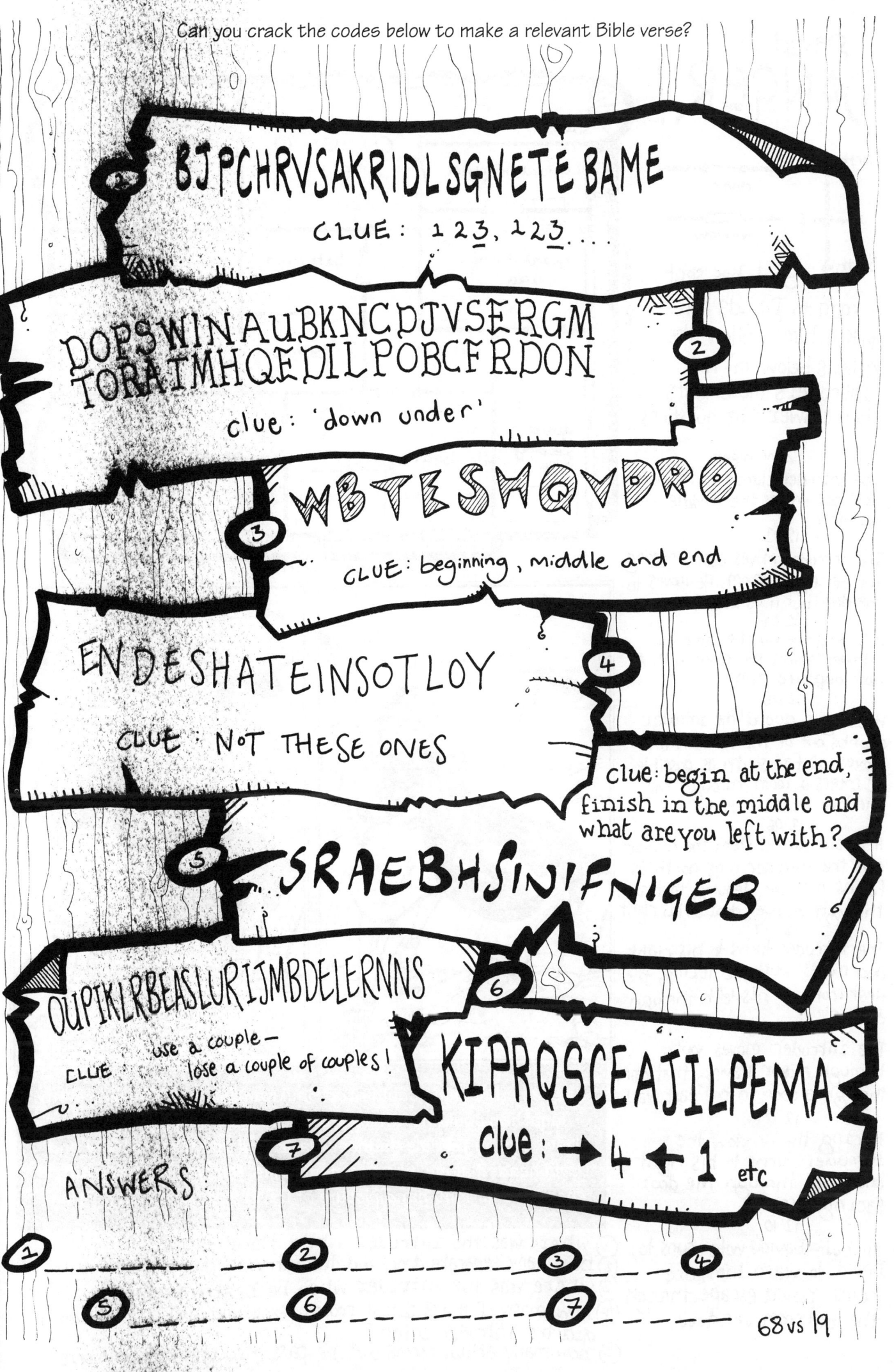

David in DANGER!

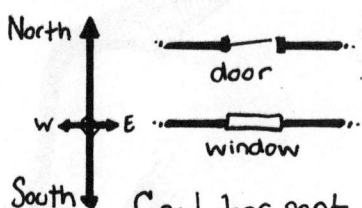

North ↑
W ←→ E
South ↓

– – – door
═══ window

Saul has sent a man to David's house to kill him! Follow the details below of the intruder's movements then answer the questions...

12 midnight
The intruder climbs up the north wall and enters the middle window.

12.02
The intruder moves east, entering the far right room. He moves to the door but it is locked.

12.04
Returning the way he came the intruder enters the room with a door opposite him.

12.05
Hearing a guard the intruder climbs out of the window and moves as far south as possible. He enters a room through the window nearest him.

12.06
A guard arrives from the corridor and the intruder runs north as far as possible, leaving that room through an open door on his right.

12.07
The intruder turns to his right and moves south, entering the first room on his left through a door.

12.08
The intruder moves south through a door leaving that room through a door in the east wall.

12.09
Facing the window the intruder turns to his right and goes through the door facing him.

12.10
Michal – David's wife – runs to David to warn him. She helps David escape through the bedroom window.

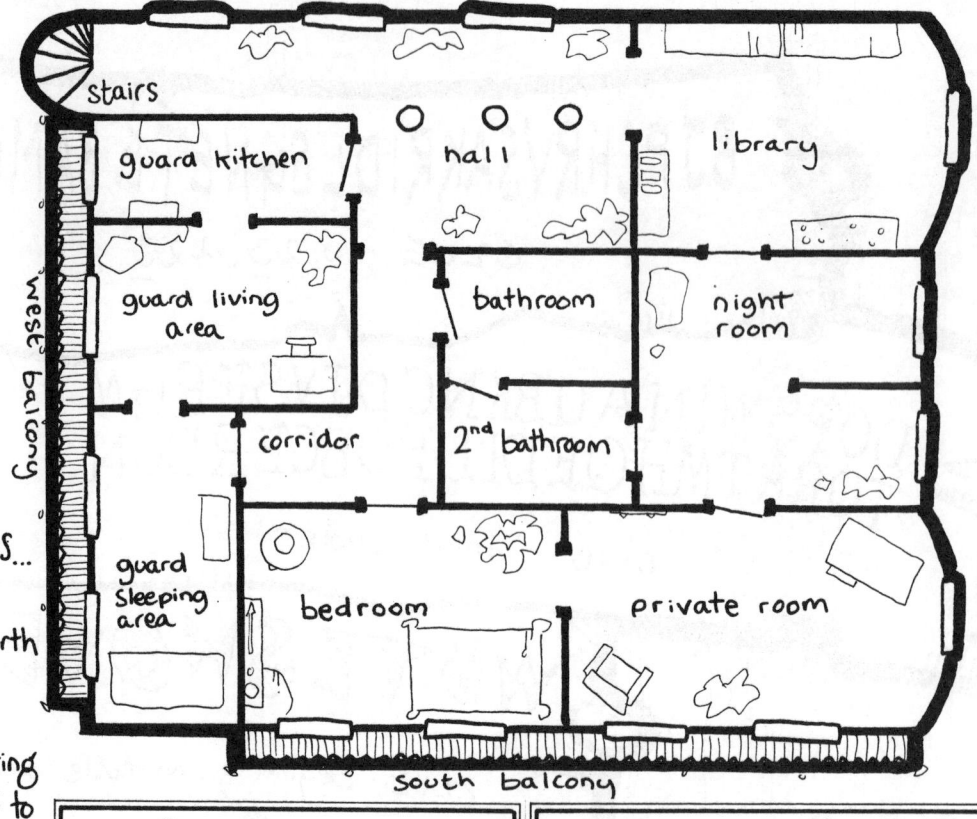

It seemed nothing could stop Saul wanting to kill David – even Jonathan could no longer protect him. David knew he had to leave. With a terrible sadness David and Jonathan parted and David headed alone into the mountains. Can you spot ten differences in the right-hand picture of David and Jonathan parting?

① Where was the intruder when David escaped?
② How many separate doors did the intruder go through?
③ Where was the intruder when he heard a guard?
④ How many of the 9 actual rooms (excluding hall and corridor) did the intruder enter?
⑤ How many actual rooms did he pass through more than once?

EPISODE 4

David Spares Saul's Life

EPISODE 4 — David Spares Saul's Life

Reading

1 Samuel 24:1-22.

Background information

David eventually settled at the cave of Adullam. When his father and brothers heard, they joined him there — as did many other people that for various reasons didn't want to live in the cities. David soon became the leader of about 400 men and they lived in the mountains being paid to protect local farmers' cattle.

Overheads

1. (Background) David and his band of men.
2. (v 4) David cuts Saul's robe.
3. (v 8) David calls out to Saul.

What this episode tells us

What we can learn from David
Confident and secure trust in God.

What we can learn about God
He will work out our problems instead of us (not yet evident in the story, but implied here and evident in the next episode).

Discussion questions and desired answers

If David knew Saul's kingship would eventually be his, why didn't he take it by killing Saul when he had the chance?
David knew that Saul was still God's anointed king for that time and God hadn't told David to kill him.

What does this tell us about David?
That he obeyed and respected God, but more, that he trusted God. Although a means to an end seemed available God hadn't said it was the way to take — David trusted that the position God wanted for him would come at the time God decided — and not when *he* decided.

David trusted God to give him the position he'd been anointed for, even so, Saul was still trying to kill David — what had David done to deserve this?
Nothing.

If you were being unfairly accused or attacked, what do you think you would want to do in David's position?
Justify yourself, put an end to it, etc.

Read Luke 6:27-29. What is Jesus saying?

That it is not up to us to retaliate or justify ourselves – we should treat people as God would, no matter how they treat us!

Read Psalm 37:3-6. What is David saying here?

David is saying that if you commit your way to God, trust in him and obey his ways, then God will be the one to put things right to justify you.

Continue the passage with verses 7-9. What does David say here?

David is saying that not only can you trust your problems or unfairness directed at you to God, but you shouldn't even let them worry or anger you! David means that our trust in God to work them out for us can be so secure and so complete that our problems will no longer worry us!

How can we have such a secure trust?

By knowing and by really believing in our heart the nature of God. When we respond to situations and to people in the way God would want us to we are acting in complete accordance with his will and he will never overlook that.

Additional material

Fun

'Snatching From Saul' Game. One person is Saul – they must either sit or stand with an assortment of objects close to them (even touching them, if desired). Everybody else must start a good five paces away from 'Saul' who should shut his eyes. People take it in turn to be David and to creep forward and take an object without Saul touching them. (Saul may not wave his hands about making it difficult – but rather should listen carefully and make a well-timed grab!) A David who is grabbed then takes over as Saul. No peeking, Sauls!

Worksheet

Self-explanatory.

Take-home sheet

Stalactites 4 and 10. Material piece no. 4.

Closing prayer

Dear Jesus, it is so good to know that you care about every situation I am in and that I need never dwell on my own fears or worries when I can entrust them to you. I pray, Lord, that I may come to know and trust you in the same way David did. Amen.

In spite of promising not to harm David it isn't long before Saul is again out to kill him. In the desert of Ziph Saul hunts David with 3000 soldiers. David sends scouts from his camp to report on Saul's movements!
Can you find a path that will take each of David's scouts to one of Saul's locations and then back to David but keeping these rules:
1. No path may be used more than once (but you can cross another path).
2. All of Saul's locations must be visited – one scout per location.
3. Each scout must return to David using a different path.

EPISODE 5

David and the Death of Saul

EPISODE 5

David and the Death of Saul

Reading

1 Samuel 29:1-11 and 31:1-8.

Background information

With Saul still hunting him down, David eventually turns to Israel's enemies, the Philistines, knowing that there, Saul will not be able to harm him. The Philistines, believing David to have turned against Israel, let him rule in a town called Ziklag. From there, David fought the Amalakites but told the Philistines he was fighting Israel. Presently the Philistine armies planned an attack against Israel and King Saul.

Overheads

1 (29:4) The Philistine leaders argue over David.
2 (29:6) Achish explains their decision to David.
3 (31:8) The Philistines find Saul's body on the battlefield.

What this episode tells us

What we can learn from David
Consistent trust and obedience leads to God acting for you.

What we can learn about God
Works for us when we obey him (but in *his* timing).

Discussion questions and desired answers

In the last episode we learnt that it was not for us to fight to prove ourselves right or to seek revenge, but we should trust our problems to God and follow his ways. How did David show that?
By not killing Saul – even though it would have brought an end to his problems.

We also learnt last week that by entrusting our problems to God and being obedient, he sorts them out for us. How is this evident in today's story?
God saw that David was removed from the battle in which Israel was defeated, therefore Saul died and God ensured that David had nothing to do with it!

When we know the end of the story it is easy to see how God sorted it out, but imagine you were David in the Philistine army; why was this such a difficult situation for him?
His obedience in not killing Saul led him to join his enemies who are now intent on killing Saul. David needs to look a part of them for his own safety!

How do you think David felt?
Compromised, trapped, etc.

David was in a hopeless situation with seemingly no way out, and it seemed his obedience had led him there! What happened?
The Philistines argued and decided David shouldn't fight with

them, so he was saved from having to fight Saul and from letting the Philistines see where his loyalties would lie.

What does this tell us about God?
God has his own ways of helping us in seemingly impossible situations.

God saved David, but not till the Philistine army had already begun to march! What does this tell us about God?
We can trust in God but we cannot expect to know how or when God will act. We should remember that we can't see the end of the story, yet God can and he knows the exact moment to step in. We must trust God no matter how the situation looks and he will not let us down.

Additional material

Take time to share experiences of God answering prayers or helping to sort out situations. Did the answer or solution happen when and how you expected and knowing the end of the story was it best how it actually happened as opposed to how you perhaps initially thought?

If relevant, perhaps pray for situations in which the children are trusting God, but may not have seen any change or had any kind of answer.

Practical demonstration

Ask a willing child to fall backwards with their eyes closed and tell them you'll catch them. This takes a definite act of blind trust on the child's part. Draw the comparison to trusting in God, that he will catch us, etc. As a variation, catch some children straight away, but allow others to fall a little further to emphasise not knowing exactly *when* God will act, just that he will. Do not try this on the children if you have any doubts about your physical strength! If necessary, rope in a strong adult to help.

Worksheet

Self-explanatory.

Take-home sheet

After the <u>battle</u>, David became <u>king</u> of a <u>town</u> in Judah. Meanwhile, Saul's fourth <u>son</u> tried to <u>rule</u> all Israel but was <u>soon</u> betrayed and <u>killed</u> by his own <u>men</u>. The people of Israel <u>came</u> to David and <u>said</u> 'you <u>be</u> our king'. David did <u>not</u> fight to <u>take</u> the kingship <u>for</u> himself. Instead he <u>trusted</u> God <u>and</u> God gave it <u>to</u> him.

The squares that are not part of the picture are C, E and F.

Closing prayer

Dear Father God, thank you that you always know exactly what is best for me. Please help me to trust in your ways, even when they may be different from how I imagined. I want to live my life trusting in your way, Lord Jesus, and not my own.
Amen.

David had kept to what he knew was right (not killing Saul) and God had solved the problem for him. Below are four stories of people who did what they knew God wanted from them even though the decision may have cost them. You can see through their obedience how God changed their situation at the last moment.

Look up the verses given and fill in the missing words – can you then find all 23 missing words in the grid.

GENESIS 22:1-19

God tested _____ by asking him to _____ his only son _____. At the last moment however, God provided a _____ instead. _____ had pleased God by proving he would not withhold even his only son from Him.

DANIEL 6:6-22.

The administrators of _____ _____ had the _____ make a rule declaring that anybody who _____ to any god be thrown into the _____ _____. _____ heard the rule but did not obey it and was put in the _____ _____. However, an _____ shut the _____ of the _____ and _____ was kept safe from harm.

ACTS 5:40 AND 12:5-8

The apostles were ordered not to speak about _____ but they continued. _____ was put in Herod's _____ but before he was to go on trial God sent an _____ to free him.

DANIEL 3: 5-6, 12, 19-27

_____ _____ set up an image of _____ that all the people were to _____, but there were three Jews – _____, _____ and _____ who would not bow down to it. The _____ had them thrown into the _____ _____ but God was pleased with the Jews and he made sure that the _____ did not burn them.

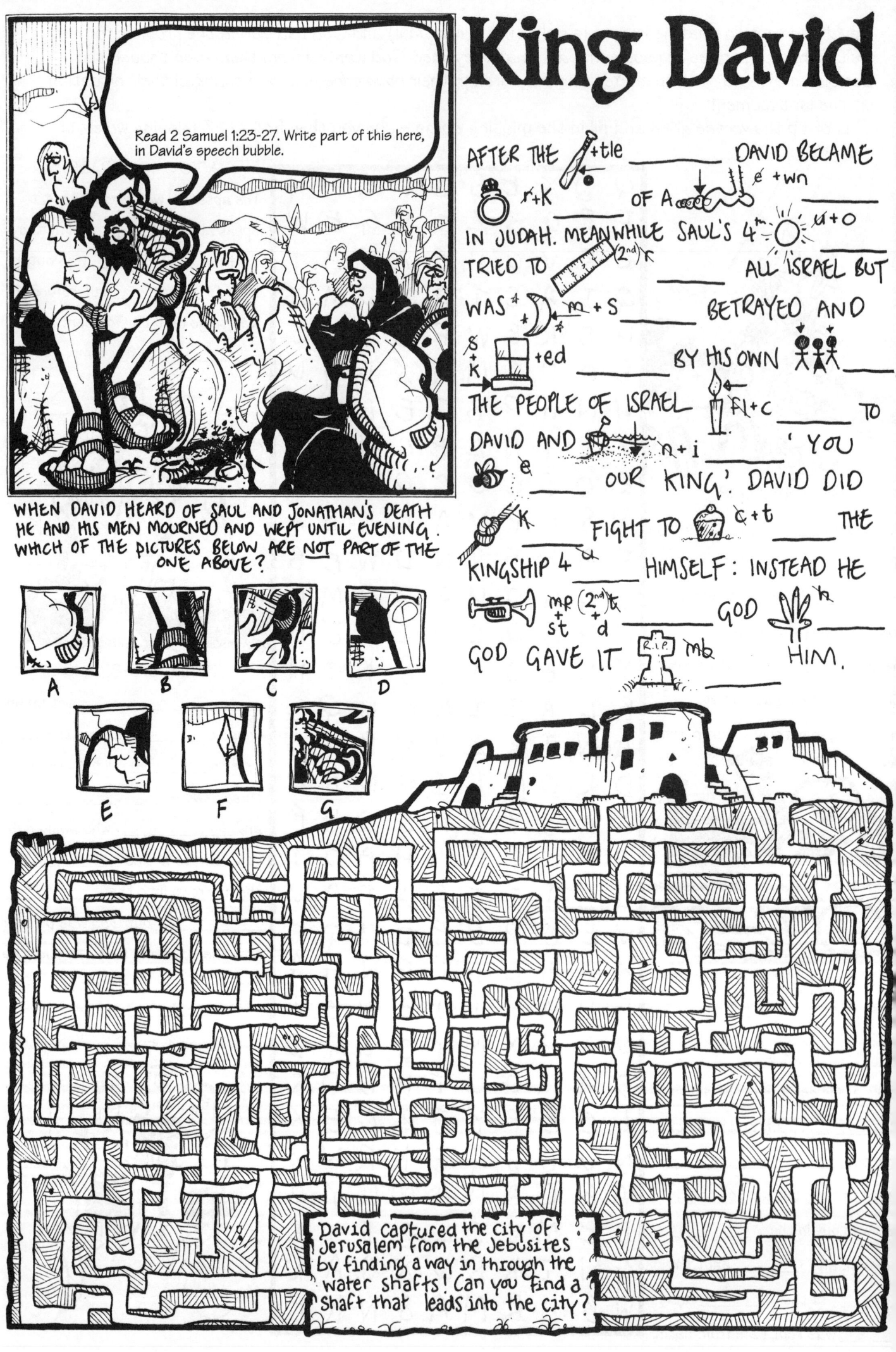

EPISODE 6

David Praises the Lord

EPISODE 6 — David Praises the Lord

Reading

2 Samuel 6:12-23.

Background information

David became king over Israel and made Jerusalem the capital city. When the Philistines heard this, they attacked David, but God was with him in his battle plans and the Philistines were defeated.

Overheads

1 (v 14) David dances with 'all his might'.
2 (v 16) Michal watches the celebrations.
3 (v 21) David confronts Michal.

What this episode tells us

What we can learn from David
Give God the praise and thanks he is due.

What we can learn about God
He is worthy of our praise simply for who he is.

Discussion questions and desired answers

What was the Ark of the Covenant?
The Ark was a sacred golden chest, the designs of which were given to Moses by God to carry the Ten Commandments. It was a symbol of God's presence and provision to the Israelites.

Why do you think the people rejoiced to have the Ark brought to Jerusalem?
The Ark would have been a very powerful symbol of God's presence coming to dwell in the city and also a declaration and sign of his blessing on them as his chosen people.

What made David dance?
David recognised that God had been incredibly faithful to him, had given him the kingship and delivered him and Israel from all their enemies. God had given David everything and David expressed his thanks and praise as well as he possibly could. He knew what God deserved and did his best to give him just that!

Why did God punish Michal?
Not just because she judged David's worship – a personal expression between him and God – but because she denied God the praise he was due at such a sacred moment.

How should we aim to be like David?
David consistently recognised what was due to God and gave it to him. In our daily lives there is always something we can praise God for.

Read Psalm 103:1-4. What reasons are there for praising God here?
Because of all he has done for us.

Read Psalm 104:1-4. What reasons are given here?
Simply because of who he is – he is God and deserves praise.

When should we praise God?
The Bible is very specific that praise is something due to God. It is not something we give if we feel like it but something he is actually *due* because of all he is.

What does it mean to praise and worship God?
People often think that it means singing hymns and praying on a Sunday, but it is not just that. Worship is a lifestyle. It is an attitude in our hearts that looks to live in a way that pleases God and to acknowledge and praise him for his provision in our lives and for all he has done for us.

Additional material

Encourage a time of giving thanks to God in prayer. Encourage the children to thank God for what they feel thankful for, not what they think they should thank him for, e.g. if a friend has become a Christian they may want to thank him, but equally as valid they may want to thank him for a fun day they had, a good film they saw, etc. A worshipful lifestyle involves God in everything, not just the spiritually significant things but our everyday activities too.

Fun '*As David Danced*' *Game.* Try a dancing competition with prizes – who can dance 'with all their might' most convincingly? Alternatively, have a wild 'musical statues' with everyone dancing mightily then attempting to hold whatever pose they happen to be in when the music stops.

Worksheet Self-explanatory. (Children should be encouraged to find a quiet spot alone if this is to be done in lesson time. If children are willing, maybe read some out but from the outset make it known their 'psalms' can remain private if they wish so as to encourage honesty.)

Take-home sheet Psalm 95:1. (Come, let us sing for joy to the Lord.)

Closing prayer

Lord God, There is not one thing that deserves my praise like you do. You are almighty God who created everything I see, everyone and everything I love. There is no one like you in all the earth and when I think that you can be so awesome and so powerful yet still want to know and love me, I am filled with wonder and thanks. Thank you, Lord. Amen.

Use the space below to write your own psalm of thanks or praise to God. Or alternatively rewrite a psalm of your choice in your own words. (Below are some psalms on various topics that you may find useful.)

General praise – Psalms 96 and 150. Thanks – Psalms 66, 100, 116.
Forgiveness – Psalm 32. Praise of God's power – Psalm 29.
God's works – Psalm 19. Praise through creation – Psalms 104 and 148.
Refuge in God – Psalm 46.

THE PRAISE DUE TO GOD!

Join up the dots to reveal the object that caused the people to praise.

Read Luke 19 vs 37-40... what are the people doing?

the Pharisees want this stopped! what does Jesus say will happen if God does not get what the people are giving him?

CAN YOU WORK OUT WHAT NATURE IS SAYING TO GOD BELOW?

Psalm 95:1

Can you spot ten differences in the lower picture of David and Michal (not including the speech bubble). Look up 2 Samuel 6:20-22 and in your own words write Michal's accusation to David and David's response in the empty speech bubbles.

EPISODE 7

God's Amazing Promise

EPISODE 7 — God's Amazing Promise

Reading

2 Samuel 7:8-16, 18-21, 27-29.

Background information

David is king over Israel and Jerusalem is established as the capital. The enemies of Israel are defeated and David's empire is now one of the strongest kingdoms of its day. David spoke to Nathan, the prophet, and told him how he wanted to do more to show his gratitude to God – perhaps build him a temple? Yet God spoke to Nathan that night and told him that instead of David doing great things for him, he wanted to do even more for David!

Overheads

1. (Background) David conferring with Nathan.
2. (v 8) God speaks to Nathan.
3. (v 18) David humbly acknowledges God's incredible blessing.

What this episode tells us

What we can learn from David
Humility – recognition of our own unworthiness and God's grace.

What we can learn about God
Amazing grace – gives us what we do not deserve.

Discussion questions and desired answers

God makes an amazing promise to David to establish his kingdom for ever and to bring blessing on him and his son who will succeed him. What had David done to deserve this?
Nothing. In spite of all the good things we have already learnt about David, it was not for what he had done that God made this promise.

Read verse 21 again. Why does David say God made this promise to him?
For the sake of his word and according to his will.

What does David mean?
He is saying that God simply chose him, not because of who he is but because of who God is.

This is an example of the grace of God. What do we mean by this?
It is when God freely gives us something we have done nothing to deserve. (The most obvious example being that he gave his own son, Jesus, to die for us when we were and are all sinners.)

God gave David kingship over an entire kingdom, yet in the same way he gave that to David (through his grace) he gives things to us, too. Can you think of some examples?
Our personal talents and abilities (encourage specifics, e.g. good

at sport, good at music, drama, art, etc.), material blessings, financial blessings, relationship blessings (e.g. a best friend, a happy home, etc.)

Is it wrong for us to know we are good at something or have something special?
Not if we understand why we have it! If God entrusts us with something it is right to acknowledge it and thank him – and enjoy it. If we remember that it is only by God's grace that we have any kind of blessing in the first place then we will not become proud of 'our' talent or 'our' things, etc. We can accept the fact that God has chosen to bless us in a particular way, but remember that it is never because we are special or great in any way, but because God is special and great.

How then should we use God's gifts?
God entrusts us with things not to bring any glory to ourselves – but to give glory to him. The most important way of making sure we do this is by looking at our heart attitude – how we really feel and think of them inside. If we never forget and are always thankful *inside*, then that will always find a way to affect how we act and what we say on the outside.

Additional material

Teaching aid

Read or improvise a story similar to the following – perhaps using relevant names or hobbies from your group:

Anna loved riding horses, then one day her best friend gave her a horse! Imagine how pleased she was and how well she groomed and looked after her horse. Her friends thought her horse was wonderful and they were so impressed when Anna told them her best friend had given it to her! She rode it every day and entered him in several competitions. After lots of training she won a very important competition and as the local newspaper photographed her, she was so proud to think how happy her best friend would be to see those photos and her stories . . .

Ask the children to make comparisons to God's gifts to us, e.g. accepted the gift thankfully, looked after the gift, used it regularly and to the best of ability, made the most of it always remembering and being thankful to her best friend – the giver, looked to please the giver with how well the gift was used, etc.

Worksheet

You will need scissors.

Take-home sheet

Matching squares: K1 and C6, K3 and I4, E2 and H6, F4 and K5.

Closing prayer

Dear God, when I look at my life and all I have, I recognise your incredible generosity to me – thank you, Lord Jesus, for everything you have entrusted to me. I pray that the way I use your gifts is pleasing to you. Please help me, Lord, to recognise your blessings all around me. Thank you so much! Amen.

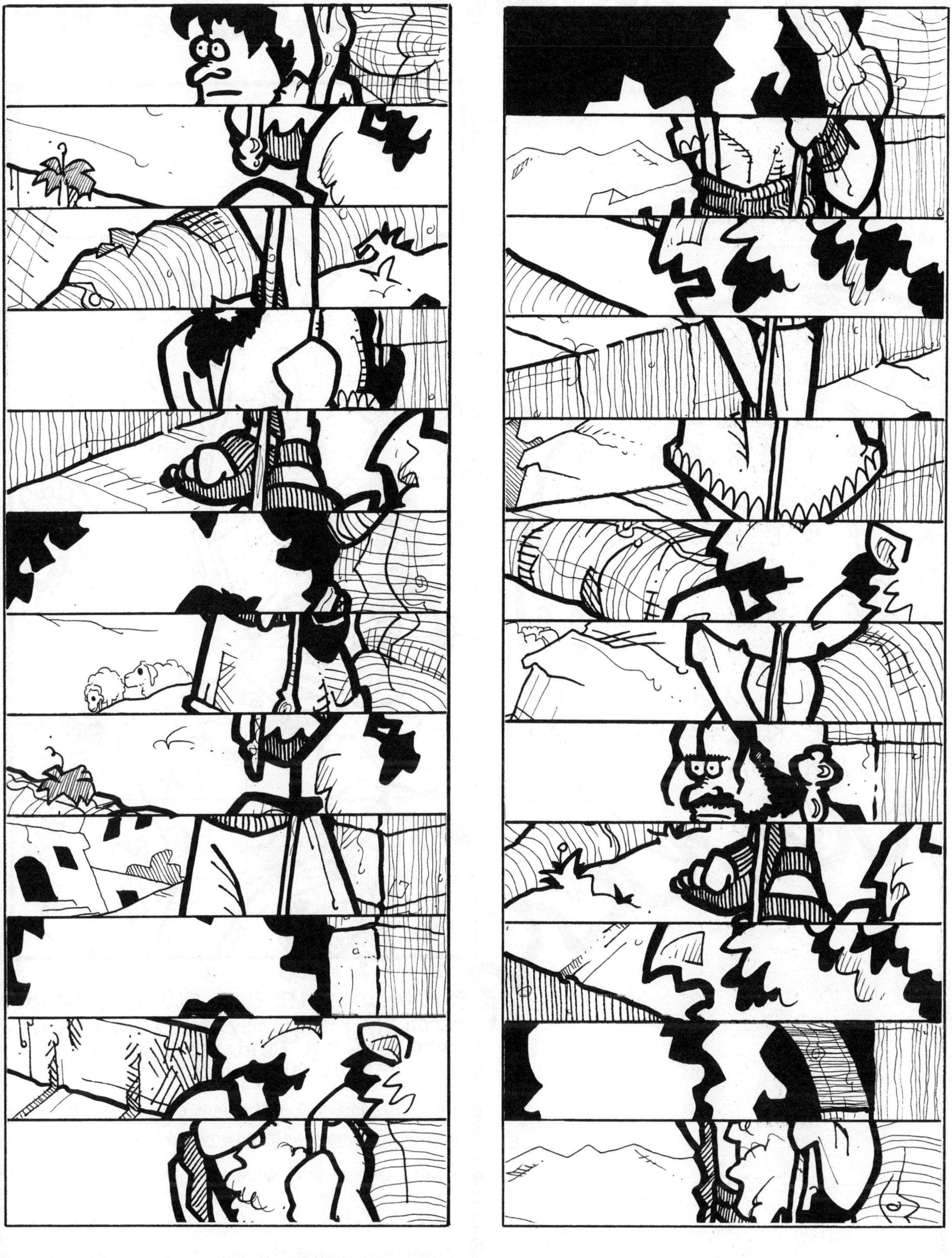

Read 2 Samuel 7:8.
Cut up the boxes above and rearrange them to show David when he was younger and where God has now brought him to.

God's promise to David

Look up Psalm 89:35-37.
Can you fill in the missing words and then find them in the word search below?

The Lord says, "I will not lie to _____ – that his _____ will _____ _____ and his _____ _____ before me like the _____; it will be _____ for ever like the _____, the _____ witness in the _____."

Four squares in the above picture are repeated identically (although they may be a different way round). Can you find the 4 sets of matching squares?

Read Luke 1:26-33. In the angel's speech bubble, write in your own words what he says to Mary in vv 31-33.

Read 2 Samuel 7:16. What does God promise David?

Remembering what the angel told Mary, who did God tell Mary that David's throne would pass to – the person who fulfils God's promise to David?

GOD MADE A PROMISE TO DAVID THAT WE KNOW HAS COME TRUE! CAN YOU WRITE OR DRAW SOMETHING GOD HAS PROMISED OR SAID TO YOU IN THIS SPACE....

EPISODE 8

David's Dreadful Sins

EPISODE 8

David's Dreadful Sins

Reading

2 Samuel 11:2-5, 14-17, 26-27, and 12:1-10, 13-14.

Background information

David's kingdom was at its strongest point ever – God had blessed him greatly. Yet with such authority there is a great responsibility.

Overheads

1 (v 2) David watches Bathsheba.
2 (v 17) Uriah dies in battle.
3 (12:7) Nathan rebukes David.

What this episode tells us

What we can learn from David

Recognition of our own sin and genuine repentance bring forgiveness.

What we can learn about God

Requires only that we are truly sorry to forgive us. Grace undeserved.

Discussion questions and desired answers

What was David's sin?

Adultery with Bathsheba and murdering Uriah through his commands.

In Episode 7 we read how richly God blessed David. What does this story teach us about David?

That in spite of everything God had done for David, he was just as liable to make a mess of things by sinning as anybody else.

What does this teach us about ourselves?

It teaches us how little we deserve what God trusts to us. David was given much and his sin was very great – yet in our own ways we all misuse what God entrusts to us.

In the last episode we looked at God's grace in blessing us when we'd done nothing to deserve it. Which verse in today's story speaks most strongly of God's grace?

Chapter 12:13; 'The Lord has taken away your sin . . .'

Why did God take away David's sin?

Read Psalm 51:1-4 (written after his sin with Bathsheba). David recognised his own sin and asked for God's forgiveness.

What is necessary for us to be forgiven?

Genuine repentance (continue Psalm 51:16-17). God doesn't require any great ritual or performance, he looks directly where he always looks – our hearts. Ask the children to think of an occasion when they've apologised over something they weren't genuinely sorry about, then compare that to a time they were genuinely sorry. God always knows what's in our hearts.

Sin is an unfortunate part of our lives, but that doesn't excuse us doing it. However, it does mean we need to recognise it and put it right. How do we do this?

As Christians, the Holy Spirit lives in our lives and will convict us of sin – this means he will bring it to our attention.

Then what must we do?

We have a choice – we can either recognise the sin and put it right (as David did) or we can try to ignore it. God's grace is there to forgive us but it is up to us to ask.

Do you think that forgiveness sounds too easy?

Yes, and it should because that is the nature of grace; it sounds too good to be true, yet is true and is always there for us!

Additional material

Lesson aid

You will need paper, rubber, pencils and blindfolds. Ask the children to begin drawing a picture. Let them draw for a little while (perhaps be specific in asking them to draw an animal, or person or whatever). As they draw, tell them that this is like their lives – the finished picture in their mind is like God's perfect way of life and their drawing is like them getting there. Now blindfold them with the 'Blindfold of Pride'! This symbolises the pride that causes us to sin and get things wrong. Ask them to continue drawing blindfolded. Holy Spirit conviction comes in the form of removing the blindfold when they can see what a mess they've made and request the 'Rubber of Grace'! Silly, but fun and gets the point across!

Worksheet

You will need Bibles and pencils and pens. Answers: Rich man – David; Poor man – Uriah; Ewe – Bathsheba.

Closing prayer

Dear Lord Jesus, thank you that your grace is always there to forgive me when I sin. I trust, Lord, that you will convict me where I do wrong and I pray that I will be open to hear and recognise your Holy Spirit inside me. Thank you for your work in my life. Amen.

TROUBLE IN DAVID'S HOUSE!

What does God look at when we come to him for forgiveness?

Colour in each shape with a dot to reveal the answer.

David was truly sorry for his sin, and truly forgiven - yet that didn't mean he escaped the consequences of his actions. The first son born to David by Bathsheba died and soon afterwards one of David's older sons, Amnon, raped Tamar - his own sister and David's daughter. Absalom, another son of David, hated Amnon for what he did and the brothers did not speak for two years!

STUDY THE PICTURE

on the right for one minute. Amnon is in the foreground with Absalom behind him and David and Tamar on the stairs. After one minute cover the picture and see if you can answer these 10 questions (do not read the questions first!!)

1. Which men had beards?
2. Was David holding a spear?
3. How many steps were there?
4. Was Absalom facing left or right?
5. How many objects were hung on the wall?
6. Was Amnon's top stripey or squared?
7. Did the man with light hair have long hair?
8. How many spears were there in the picture?
9. What was to the left behind Absalom?
10. Were the walls made of wood or stone?

After two years Absalom could contain his hatred for Amnon no longer so he murdered his brother and fled to Geshur. Can you find the route he took to get there?

EPISODE 9

David and Absalom

EPISODE 9   David and Absalom

Reading

2 Samuel 15:13-14, 17, 24-26.

Background information

Absalom stayed in Geshur for some time before David had him brought back to Jerusalem. The king and his son did not see each other even then and Absalom began to plot against David. In the morning he would wait at the city gates and speak to people that had a complaint against the king, offering them his support. In that way Absalom won many followers and after four years he went to Hebron and declared his opposition to the royal throne.

Overheads

1 (Background) Absalom gains followers outside Jerusalem.
2 (v 17) King David and the people leave Jerusalem.
3 (v 25) David tells Zadok to return the Ark.

What this episode tells us

What we can learn from David
Valuing God's will above everything else – placing God first.

What we can learn about God
Wants to be first in our hearts.

Discussion questions and desired answers

What is David doing in this episode?
He is leaving Jerusalem – in effect, allowing Absalom to take over the kingdom.

Why do you think David leaves Jerusalem?
David never fought to take the kingdom – God sovereignly gave it to him – in the same way he does not fight to keep it but would rather give God the freedom to have his will, i.e. if it is God's will that David still rules as king then God will ensure that happens – David will not try and 'force God's hand'.

Why does David send the Ark back?
By keeping the Ark, David would still be holding on to a vital part of the kingdom – the Ark was a powerful symbol to the Israelites and without it they truly were at the mercy of God. David knew either he gave *everything* up or nothing. He chose to give everything.

Do you think it could have been easy to do what David did?
Not at all! We naturally want what is best for us – David could not have wanted to lose the kingdom or to die but he would rather risk all to be sure he was where God wanted him.

Read Matthew 22:36-37. What does Jesus say?
To love God with all you have is the most important commandment.

How is this relevant to today's story?
If we truly love God as Jesus commands then he will always be our first priority – nothing should become more important to us than God and doing what he wants. What is the point of going against God's will – he knows what is best for us and like David, we need to trust him and never hold onto anything so tightly we couldn't do what God wants.

David gave the kingdom up without God even asking him to – he so much wanted to do God's will. Is there anything in your life you couldn't give up if God asked you?
Allow for a time of reflection if necessary. It is important to emphasise that God doesn't simply take away the things we enjoy – the 'things' themselves are often irrelevant – what is important is the value we place on them. If we value anything higher than God, we may well find God will test on it – there shouldn't be anything in our hearts that comes before God.

Additional material

Further reading

Genesis 22:1-14. Abraham is prepared to give up his only son for God – God tests his heart and sees that he places God first. God does not let him give up Isaac.

Fun

'Get to Absalom' Game. You will need a reasonable amount of space, preferably outdoors. Select one person to be David and one to be Absalom. The object is for the other children (the 'citizens of Israel') to start some way off from Absalom and make it to him without David spotting them. If David spots them, they are out. Start by David counting to 100 with his eyes closed. He may then look about him to see if he can see anyone and should call out their name and exact whereabouts if he can. If he is right, that person is out. After a short period, David must again cover is eyes and now count to ten. The hiding children will need to try and spot when he is counting so they can move closer to Absalom. Absalom may signal to them or talk if he desires. The winner is the last person to be seen or to make it to Absalom. David must keep having the ten-second counting times at regular intervals to give the children a chance. (Alternatively, the teacher could decide and tell David when he must count – e.g. every 30 seconds, every time they signal, etc.)

Worksheet

Self-explanatory.

Take-home sheet

'God confused Absalom's battle plans by making the good ideas of his men sound bad, and the bad ideas seem good.'

Closing prayer

Father God, I know that you are not a cruel God who wants me to give up the things I enjoy, but I understand that you do not want any of those things to ever be more important to me than you. Please look at my heart, Lord Jesus, and if I hold anything too close or too tightly, help me to recognise it so I can set it right. Thank you, Lord. Amen.

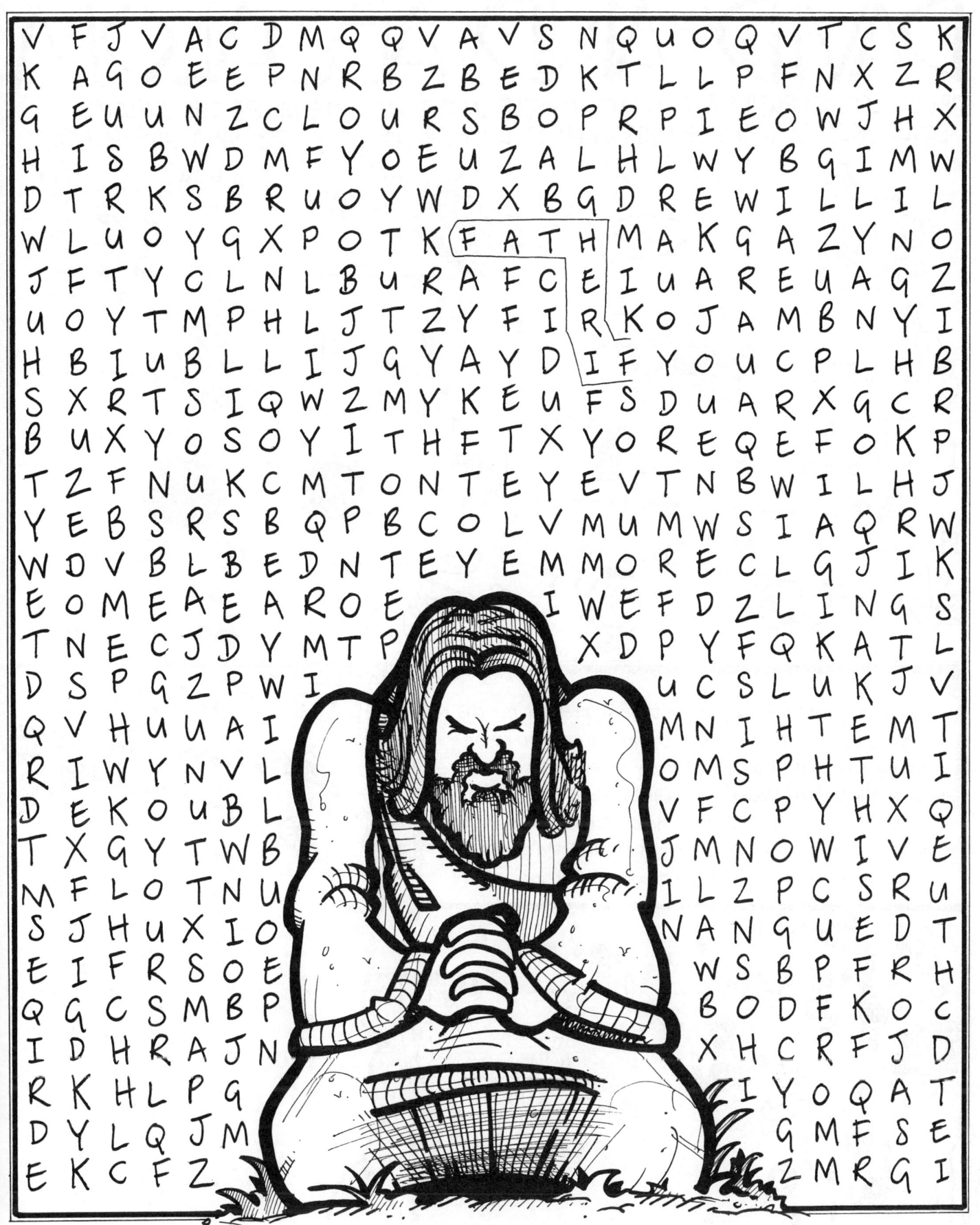

When Jesus was waiting in the garden for the soldiers to come and take him to be put on trial he prayed to his Father.
Read Luke 22:42. Can you find the words Jesus prayed in a continuous line in the grid above? The line has been started for you. (Words may go in all directions except diagonally.)

DAVID AND ABSALOM

DAVID LEFT JERUSALEM AND PUT HIMSELF IN A POSITION WHERE THE OUTCOME COULD ONLY BE GOD'S — NOT HIS OWN! FILL IN THE WORDS TO SEE WHAT HAPPENED....

Absalom gave David too much time to prepare for the battle so when he attacked, David's army was much stronger than it should have been! Below is a bird's-eye view of the battle. Using only ruler straight lines, can you join all the dots together in one continuous line that does not cross itself but separates all David's men on one side and all Absalom's on the other?

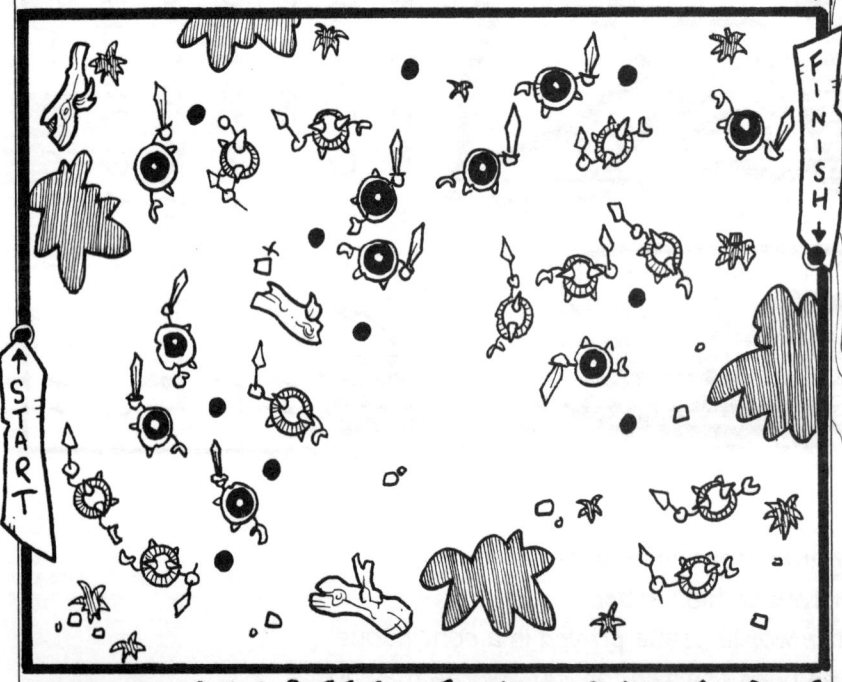

READ ABOUT THE BATTLE OUTCOME IN 2 SAMUEL 18:1-8

Join the dots to reveal: **THE FATE OF ABSALOM!!**

Read the story in 2 Samuel 18 vs 9 & 15

EPISODE 10

David and the Temple

EPISODE 10

David and the Temple

Reading

1 Chronicles 28:2-12 and 19.

Background information

Although Absalom was dead, David was extremely sad – he hadn't wanted his son to die, even if it meant an end to the rebellion. David eventually returned as king to Jerusalem and although there were people that still weren't happy with his rule, they became fewer and fewer. As David grew older, God began to show him designs for the temple that was to be built in Jerusalem. Under inspiration from God, David designed and planned the temple and when the time came for him to pass his kingship to Solomon (his son by Bathsheba) he summoned all the officials of Israel to hear what he would say.

Overheads

1 (Background) David plans for God's temple.
2 (v 2) David addresses Israel.
3 (v 11) The temple plans are given to Solomon.

What this episode tells us

What we can learn from David
A holy life is a result of our choices.

What we can learn about God
He blesses our obedience and disciplines our disobedience.

Discussion questions and desired answers

David was publicly handing his kingship to his son Solomon. What is the main advice he chooses to give to him at such an important moment? (See verse 8)
To willingly and honestly follow God's commands.

What do we know from David's life is a result of disobeying God's commands?
Discipline – although there may always be forgiveness, there is still discipline and the consequences of disobedience. (Recap on these in David's life if necessary, such as the violence in his household/family, death of his baby son, rebellion, etc.)

How do we live according to God's commands? (Read Psalm 101:3-4)
It is based on the choices we make – David says here that he will choose to live a holy life – at any moment in any decision, we can choose God's way or our way.

Do you think choosing God's way is easy?
No, it is not! We are constantly tempted and constantly fail.

How can we be sure God knows how hard it is to live how he desires? (Read Hebrews 4:15)
He (Jesus) understands and sympathises with us, because he was tempted just like us!

This means that God knows how difficult the temptations we face are. He knows how easy or how hard we fall. What does David say is the result of keeping God's commandments?
Blessing and closeness to God – relationship, etc.

How do we know that in David's last years he was close to God?
His time was spent with God speaking so clearly to him he was able to plan and design the entire temple!

Can we hear God in this way too?
Yes! Drawing close to him and keeping his commands means that we come to recognise him much more clearly in what we do. And in the same way he helped David create the temple, so he can help us in our lives with everything that we do.

Additional material

Discussion/writing

Ask the children to imagine that they are David about to hand over the kingship to Solomon in front of all Israel's officials. Based on their experience and what they know to have been true in their lives, what is the most important piece of advice they would give him? Encourage them to be honest to their experience, rather than to copy David, because they think it's the right answer. Point out that there is no right or wrong answer. Now ask them to write down their thoughts. If relevant read some out to the group (use discretion and recognise that some children will not write honestly if their answer is to be read out).

Worksheet

You will need scissors for this.

Take-home sheet

Puzzle: Gold 5 talents, Iron 100 talents, Bronze 20 talents, and Silver 5 talents.
Jewel piles C and D are identical.

Closing prayer

Dear Lord Jesus, I want to live in a way pleasing to you. I pray that when I make my decisions, you will guide me and give me the necessary strength to always take your ways instead of my own. Thank you, Lord, that you want to be as close to me as you were to David. Please help me to recognise you in my life wherever I go, in whatever I do. Amen.

PREPARING FOR THE TEMPLE!

The Spirit of God directed David to create the entire plans for the temple his son Solomon was to build. Look at the idea for one of the temple rooms on the right. The room should be symmetrical but there are ten differences on the right-hand side. Can you find them?

The people of Israel so supported the building of the temple that they gave willingly all they could afford to help build it. Can you work out from the question below how much of each metal the people gave?

The number of talents of gold multiplied by the number of talents of silver is only half the amount of talents in iron - the full amount being five times more than the twenty talents of bronze and ten times more than the total amount of silver.

___ talents of gold ___ talents of iron
___ talents of bronze ___ talents of silver

The people also gave piles of precious stones for the building of the temple. Which two piles below are identical?

A B C
D E F

Read 1 Chronicles 28:9. Write in your own words what David said to Solomon.

Finish the David story by reading 1 Chronicles 29:23-28.

EPISODE 11

What We Have Learned from David

EPISODE 11 What We Have Learned from David

Lesson summary

This lesson is a review of what has been covered in the previous episodes, with extra game and worksheet pages instead of the usual overheads.

Discussion questions and desired answers

There are so many things we can learn from David. Bearing in mind the previous episodes, read Psalm 34. What do verses 1-3 remind us about praising God?

Praise is something God deserves. It is right for us to recognise God's provision and blessing in our lives and for our hearts always to be in an attitude of praise and thankfulness.

What does verse 4 remind us about trusting God?

We can entrust our fears and our worries to God – let them be his to sort out and not ours to worry over.

What does verse 5 remind us about forgiveness?

Sin always brings guilt and shame to us, but David reminds us that the way to remove it is to look to God. When we recognise and repent of *any* sin – no matter how great or small – God will always forgive us and take the sin clean away!

What do verses 9 and 10 tell us about putting God first?

When God is first and foremost in our lives, we will lack nothing! We are not half as aware of our own needs as we think we are, yet God knows them completely and when his will is our first priority, he will see that all other kinds of needs are sorted out.

Read verse 9 again. David talks about the importance of 'fearing the Lord' a lot in the Psalms. What do you think he means by that?

To fear the Lord does not mean to be *frightened* of him, rather to recognise exactly who he is and what our response to him should be, i.e. as well as being a God who desires friendship and intimacy with us, he is an awesome and holy God who deserves our praise, our reverence, who desires a standard of living in our lives. We should never overlook God's glory when we focus on his intimacy, and never forget the price he paid when we come to him for forgiveness.

How can we tell that David 'feared the Lord'?

We always see in David someone who recognised and did his best to meet God's standards. That which offended God, offended David (ask for examples: Goliath's blasphemy, Michal's judgement, etc.)

He knew to trust God completely (not killing Saul, leaving Jerusalem for Absalom, etc.).

He knew when to praise and thank God (dancing before the Ark, receiving the Davidic Covenant, etc.).

He always recognised his own unworthiness (his sin with Bathsheba, the covenant, etc.)

What do you think is the most important lesson to learn about God through the stories of David?

God looks at who we are inside, not outside. He sees the true motives and attitudes behind every action, and will treat us according to what our motives truly are – blessing for obedience, and discipline for disobedience.

Additional material

Fun

'Guess Again' Game. Much like Charades. It may be advisable to copy the scenes and people to be acted or described on to separate pieces of card to be handed to the children on their turn. The only other thing you may need is a timer, although props can be added to the acting scenes if desired.

Draw a scene

On page 90 you will find an empty scroll. Use this for the children to draw (or write as a non-artistic alternative!) their favourite scene from the David story. You may like to make this into a competition with prizes for the best/most creative or to display them in the church so that everyone can see what the children have been working on in the past weeks. This could be carried out in lesson time or at home.

Take-home sheet

This week's take-home sheet is a double page spread board game for two or three players and a page of game rules.

Closing prayer

Dear Father God, thank you for all the things I have learnt about David. I pray, Lord, that you will help me work these things into my own life and where difficult choices and temptations face me, I pray, Lord, that you will help me to be strong and keep my eyes on you. I ask these things in Jesus' name. Amen.

Siege

This is a game for two or three players.

You will need

Two dice. Plenty of small objects to use as counters, such as buttons, seeds and pennies, for example.

Object of the game

To occupy Jerusalem and defeat all of your opponents.

To begin

Each player has five counters. These represent five armies and should be placed on the start squares. Roll one dice to determine who goes first.

Moving about the board

Each player throws both dice and moves either one army the total throw, or divides the amount among as many armies as they choose. For example, a roll of 9 could move one army nine spaces, or three armies three spaces. The total amount of each throw *must* be used, and retracing steps to use up the total roll is *not* allowed!

Battle

To go into battle, you must land on the same square as your enemy. The attacker and the defender then roll one dice each, at the same time. The winner is the player with the highest score and the loser must take their army out of the game. In the event of a draw, the players roll again.

You may attack or defend with more than one army provided all armies are on the same square. When fighting with more than one army, continue rolling the dice until there is a winner.

Entering Jerusalem

When Jerusalem is unoccupied, players must roll an odd number (total of both dice) to enter. Once a player has already entered the city they may move to any entrance (without a dice roll – all the city counts as one square) and defend that entrance under normal battle rules (as above).

Additional armies

At the beginning of a turn a player receives one extra army which begins on the board on the start square, until they have an army inside Jerusalem in which case they receive two extra armies at the beginning of each turn that may enter the board directly into Jerusalem.

Extra armies can also be obtained by landing on a *star circle*. One army is awarded each time a player lands on a star circle – the extra army entering the board on that particular circle.

From the first moment a player has *all* their armies inside Jerusalem, no extra armies are awarded to anyone – either at the beginning of turns or from landing on star circles.

Winning the game

To win the game, all of your opposing players' armies must be defeated.

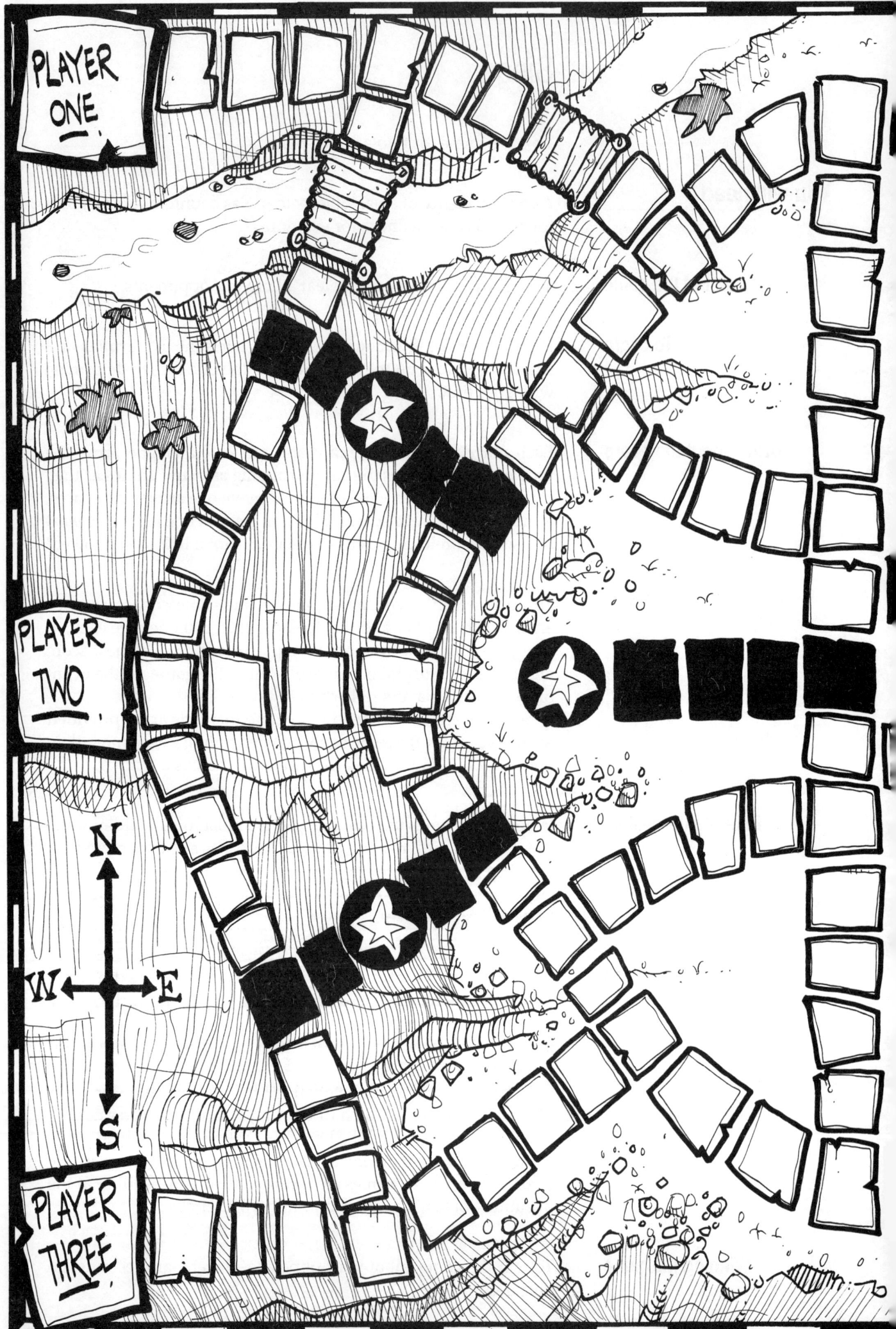

Guess Again! A group game

Before beginning the game, you will need to make the following sets of cards. There are nine under *Acting*, and eleven under *Describing*.

Acting

(The actor may tell their own team if they are acting either a Person or a Scene.)

Person
1. David
2. Goliath
3. Saul
4. Michal

Scene
5. Samuel anoints David
6. David dances before the Ark
7. David cuts a piece out of Saul's cloak
8. Saul throws his spear at David as he plays
9. David and Goliath, David gives the temple plans to Solomon.

Describing

Person
1. Samuel: *old, oil, anoint, prophet, man.*
2. Goliath: *giant, tall, Philistine, killed, stones.*
3. Jonathan: *friend, Saul, son, best, David.*
4. Absalom: *son, David, rebellion, killed, brother.*
5. Solomon: *son, David, king, temple, plans.*
6. Saul: *spear, king, David, Jonathan, kill.*

Scene
7. David dances before the Ark: *dancing, ark, might, David, Michal, Jerusalem.*
8. Saul tries to spear David: *spear, Saul, harp, singing, David, kill.*
9. David spares Saul in the cave: *cave, David, Saul, cut, knife, cloak.*
10. God's promise/covenant to David: *God, promise, David, covenant, throne, kingdom.*
11. Samuel anoints David: *Samuel, young, David, oil, anoint, prophet.*

Playing the game

Divide into two teams (A and B) and select a player to start from team A. Shuffle the cards and allow the first person to pick one. There are two types of card:

Acting These scenes or people must be acted using no dialogue. Syllable breakdown and 'sounds like' (as in *Give Us A Clue*) are permissible.

Describing The scene or person must be described without using any of the disallowed words (in italic). (The teacher should watch the card over the player's shoulder to look out for such words.) In the event a disallowed word is used, the other team gets 1 point.

Guessing

Team members may call out guesses at any time. The opposing team can confer among themselves and should the first team fail to guess in the allotted time, the opposing team may decide on one answer. In the event they too give the wrong answer, it is their turn, and neither team gets a point.

Time points

Choose a reasonable time limit to suit the children (e.g. 30/60 seconds). Two points for each correct guess. One point if opposing team use a disallowed word.

Making a Plan

1

2

4

5

7

8

10

11

Look at photographs 1 and 2.
The helicopter is on the ground
in front of the church.
The men are going to take
photographs of the village.
The cartographer, in photograph 3,
is going to make plans of the village.

3

The helicopter is hovering at
100 metres over the church.
Photograph 5 was taken from this
height. From this photograph the plan
in picture six was drawn to a scale
of approximately 1 centimetre to
four metres.

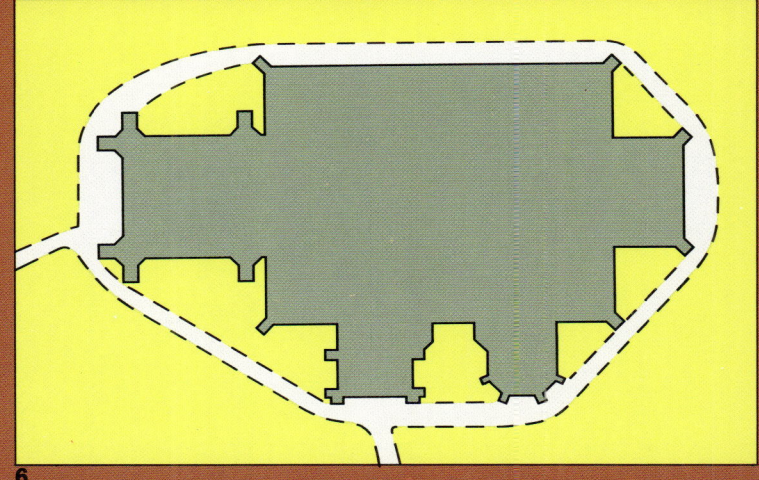
6

The helicopter, still flying above
the church, has now gone up to 300
metres. You can see the church, the
Manor House, and part of a street.
The plan in picture nine was made
from this photograph.

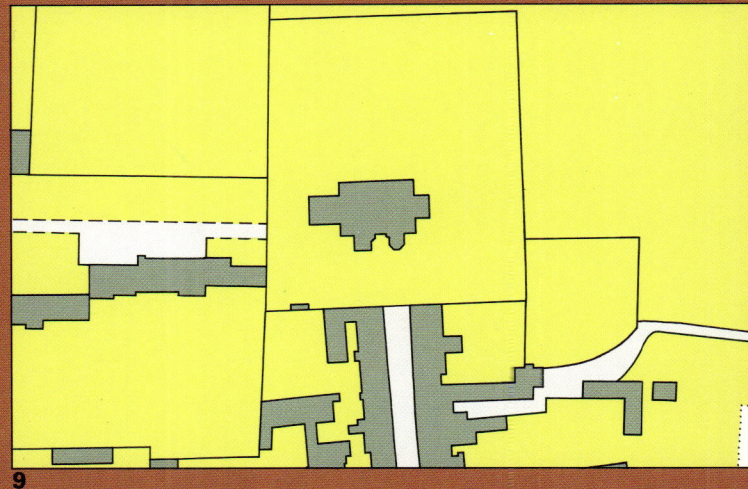
9

Photograph 11 was taken from a height
of 1000 metres. The helicopter taking
this photograph is marked by the arrow.
Note how the scale of the three
plans changes.

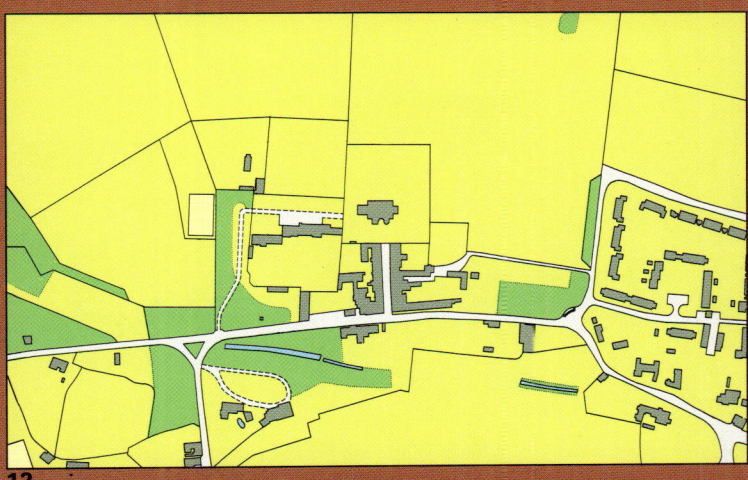
12

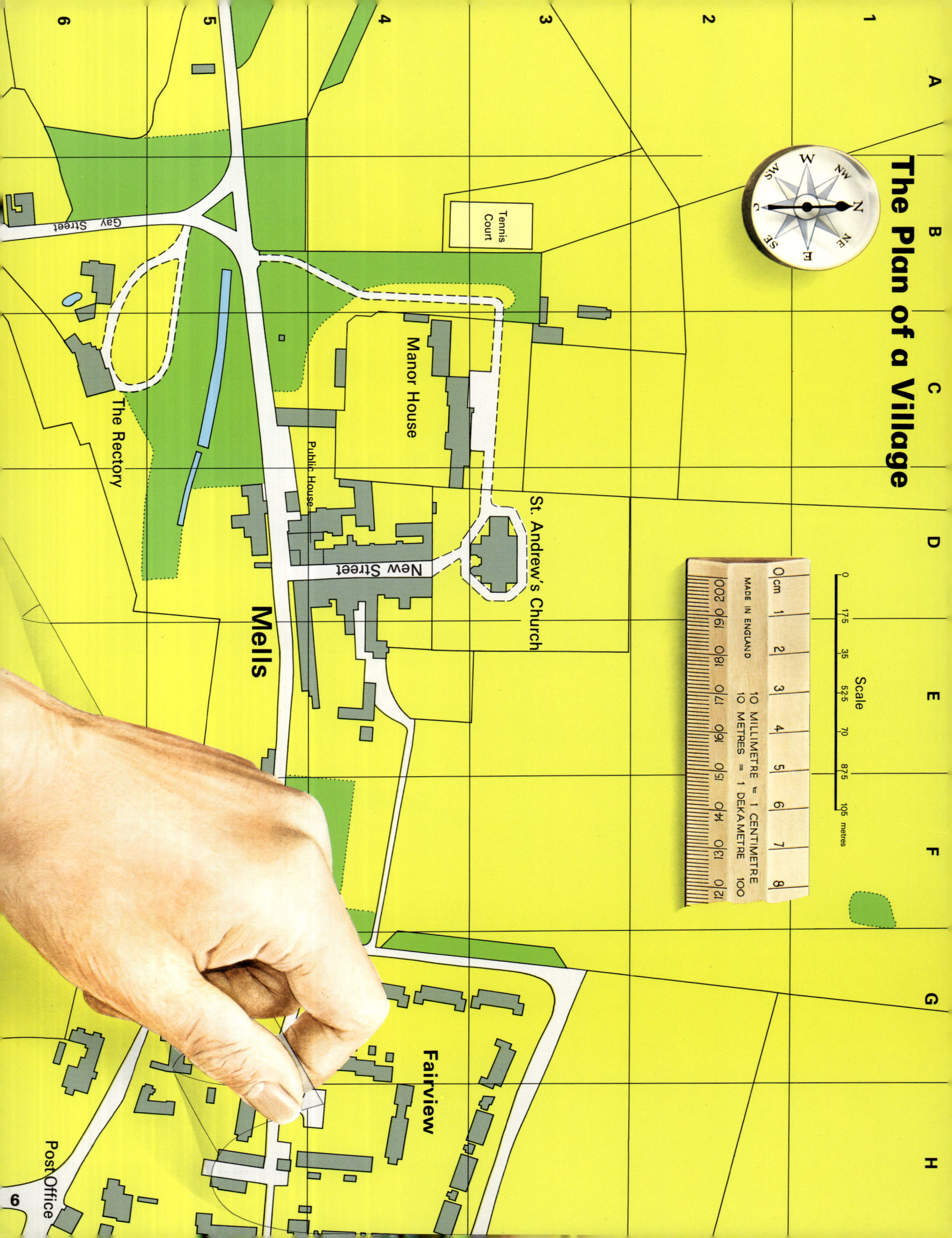

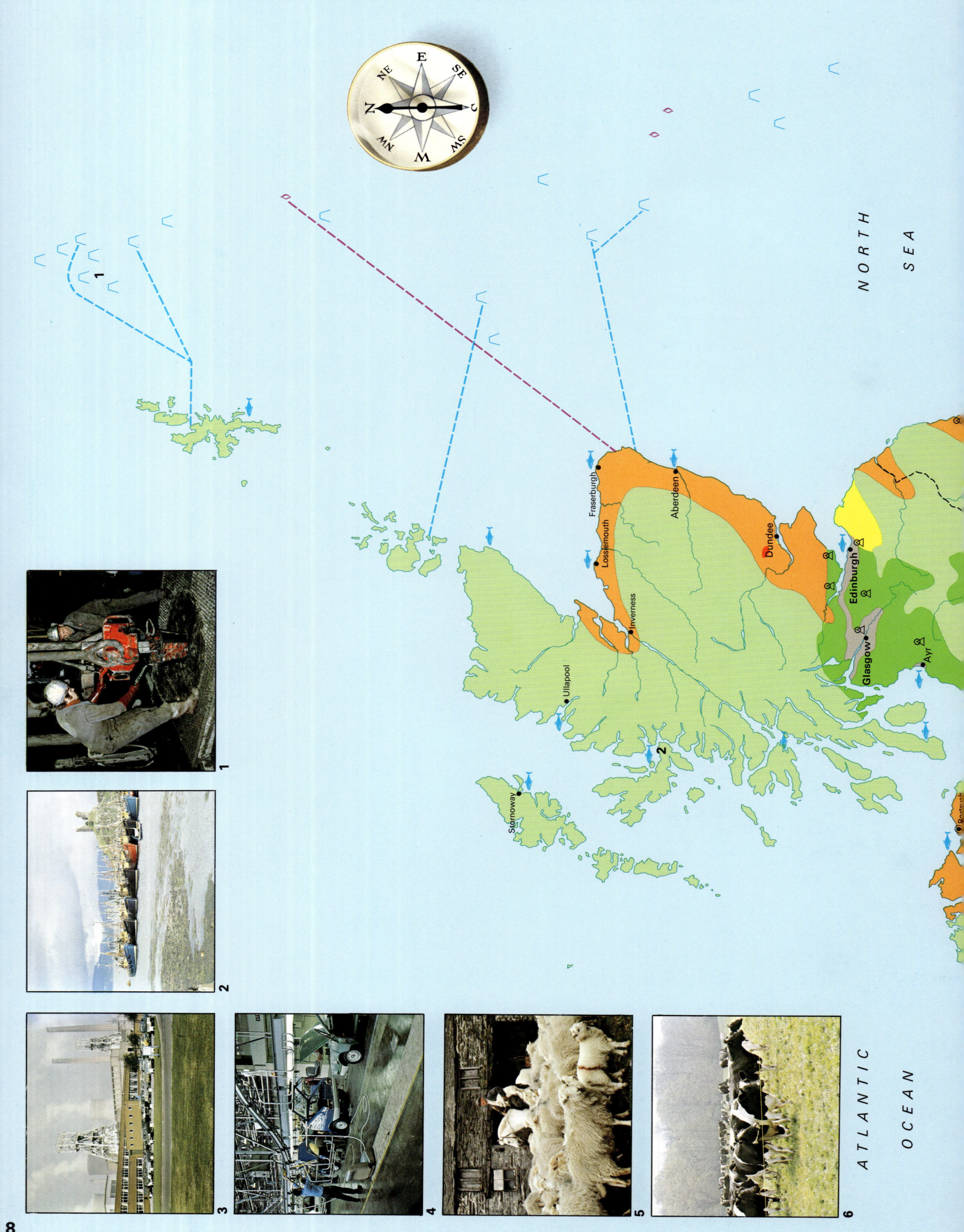

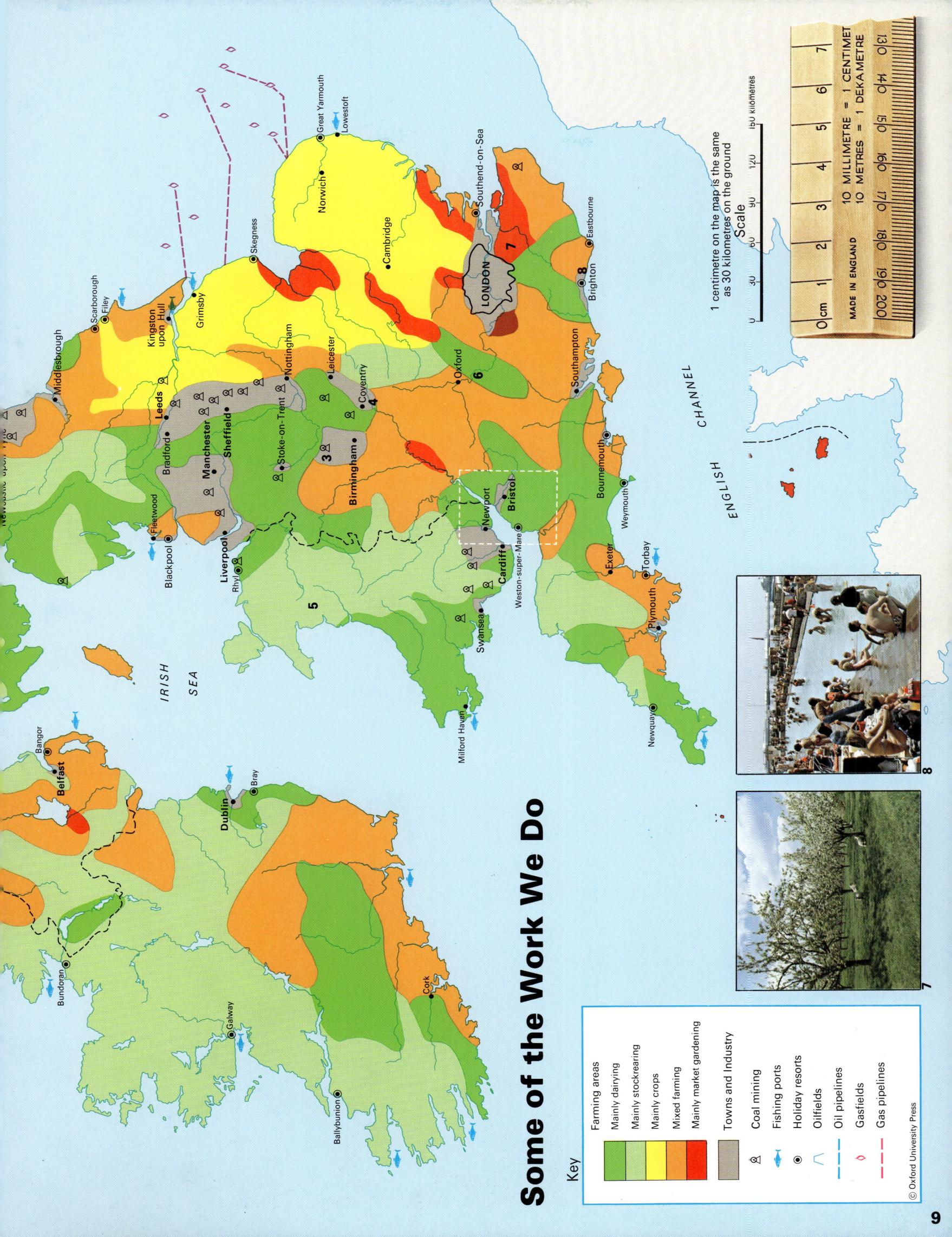

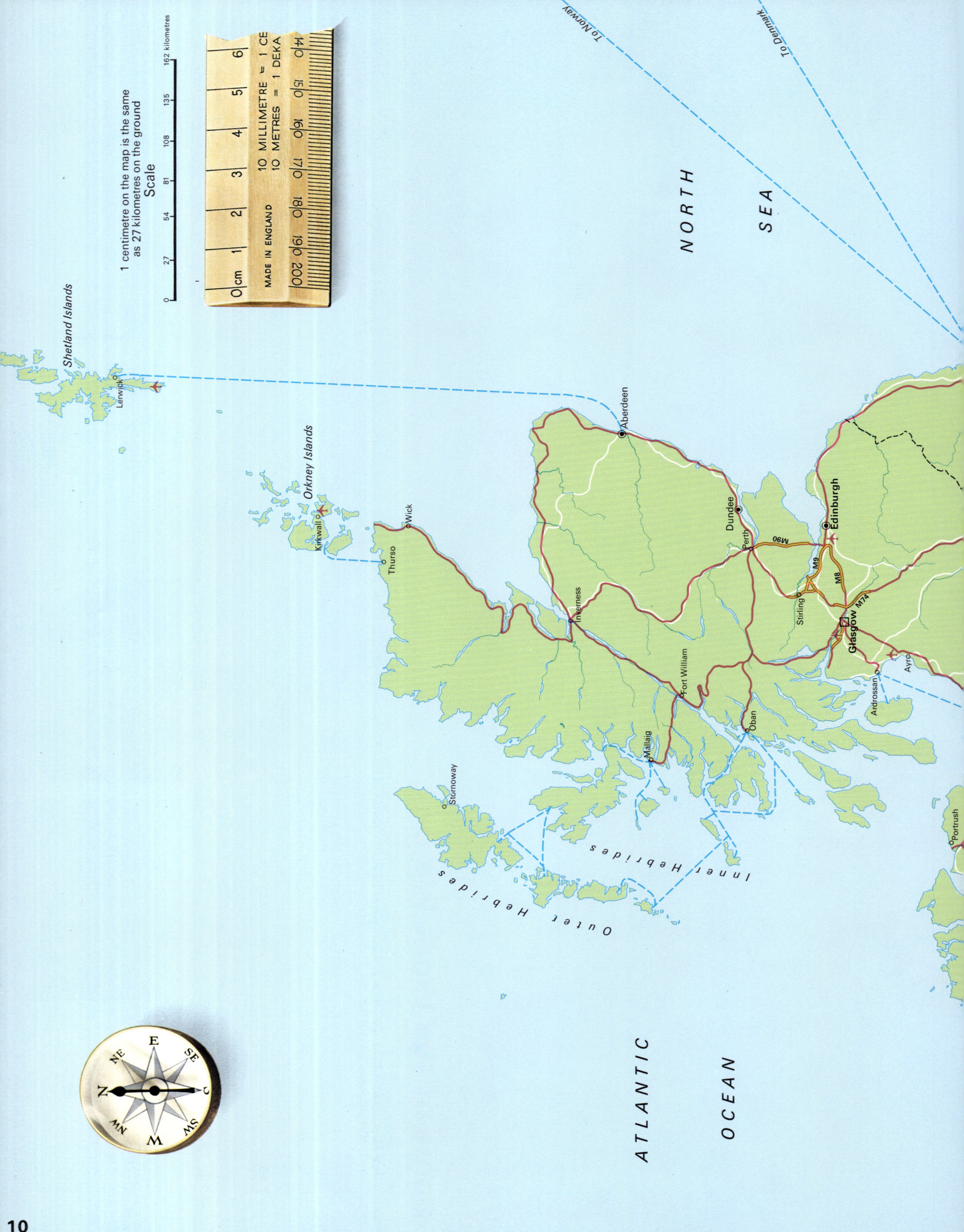

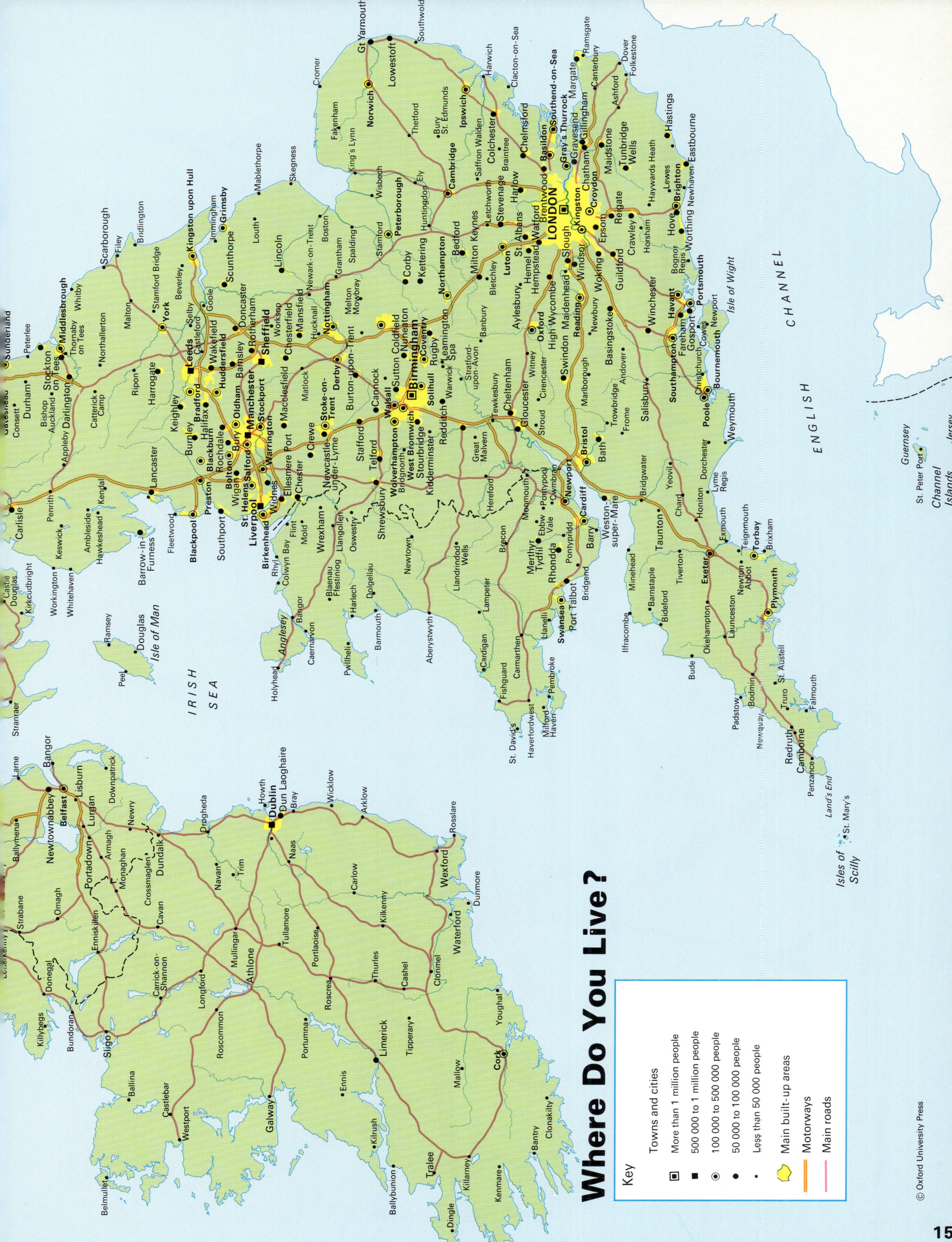